Human Resource Management

:: Author ::

Nilamben H. Sondarva

(M.COM.,B.ed., SLET)

PUBLISHED BY

The New ERa International Publishing House
HQ. At & Po. Chaveli., Ta- Chansma,
Dist- Patan, North Gujarat, India, Asia.
www.iphouseindia.com

First Publication: 29TH January, 2015

ISBN:- 978-15-08712-19-0

Price: Rs.750/- INDIA

$ 15 OUTSIDE INDIA

PUBLISHED BY

The New ERa International Publishing House
HQ. At & Po. Chaveli., Ta- Chansma,
Dist- Patan, North Gujarat, India, Asia.
www.iphouseindia.com

Contents

CHAPTER – 1
INTRODUCTION OF HUMAN RESOURSE MANAGEMENT

Human resource management (HRM) is the governance of an organization's employees. HRM is sometimes referred to simply as human resources (HR).A company's human resources department is responsible for creating, implementing and/or overseeing policies governing employee behaviour and the behaviour of the company toward its employees. Human resources are the people who work for the organization; human resource management is really employee management with an emphasis on those employees as assets of the business. In this context, employees are sometimes referred to as human capital. As with other business assets, the goal is to make effective use of employees, reducing risk and maximizing return on investment. Areas of HRM oversight include – among many others -- employee recruitment and retention, exit interviews, motivation, assignment selection, labor law compliance, performance reviews, training, professional development, mediation, and change management.

Human Resource Management

Human resource management (HRM, or simply HR) is the management of an organization's workforce, or human resources.It is responsible for the attraction, selection, training, assessment, and rewarding of employees, while also overseeing organizational leadership and culture, and ensuring compliance with employment and labor laws. In circumstances where employees desire and are legally authorized to hold a collective bargaining agreement, HR will also serve as the company's primary liaison with the employees' representatives (usually a labor union).

HR is a product of the human relations movement of the early 20th century, when researchers began documenting ways of creating business value through the strategic management of the workforce. The function was initially dominated by transactional work such as payroll and benefits administration, but due to globalization, company consolidation, technological advancement, and further research, HR now focuses on strategic initiatives like mergers and acquisitions, talent management, succession planning, industrial and labor relations, and diversity and inclusion In startup companies, HR's duties may be performed by trained professionals. In larger companies, an entire functional group is typically dedicated to the discipline, with staff specializing in various HR tasks and functional leadership engaging in strategic decision making across the business. To train practitioners for the profession, institutions of higher education, professional associations, and companies themselves have created programs of study dedicated explicitly to the duties of the function. Academic and practitioner organizations likewise seek to engage and further the field of HR, as evidenced by several field-specific publications.

The Four Basic Skills of Human Resource Management

Human resource (HR) management is a vital part of your company. To be truly effective, your human resource team must be experts in a number of important areas. The HR team is responsible for diverse aspects of each employee's career, from recruitment to hiring to various aspects of their job while employed at your company. An effective human resource team effectively executes your policies and procedures and keeps your workforce motivated and productive.

Hiring and Recruitment

Your human resource manager must be adept at hiring and recruiting new employees. Identifying, recruiting, interviewing and hiring high-performing employees is essential for the long term success of your company. Creating policies and procedures for the hiring and recruiting process and teaching these skills to all of your managers is also critical for the future of your organization.

Compensation and Benefits

Human resource managers must also create, administer and improve your compensation and benefit structures. Retaining excellent associates depends on many factors. Outstanding pay and benefits are two critical factors that will ultimately determine how well your employees feel about your organization and the likelihood that they will remain with your company in the future. Crafting an effective compensation system and determining the best benefits package for all of your employees are skills that are mandatory for your HR manager.

Training and Development

Training and development skills are also vital assets for your human resource manager. The ability to create training programs that solve human performance problems will yield important benefits for your organization. Instructional design skills, as well as outstanding facilitation and presentation abilities, result in training programs that produce tangible results for your company. Talents in program evaluation and employee feedback are also needed to constantly improve the quality of all of your training programs.

Performance Management

The ability to effectively manage the performances of your employees is an integral part of your human resource manager's job duties. Establishing and implementing a complete performance improvement process is an essential skill. Designing your performance review process, maintaining it and effectively monitoring its implementation are challenging tasks. Coaching your managers on how to use your performance management program is also an important function of your HR team.

Human resource management (HRM), or human resource development, entails planning, implementing, and managing recruitment, as well as selection, training, career, and organizational development initiatives within an organization.

The goal of HRM is to maximize the productivity of an organization by optimizing the effectiveness of its employees while simultaneously improving the work life of employees and treating employees as valuable resources. Consequently, HRM encompasses efforts to promote personal development, employee satisfaction, and compliance with employment-related laws.

To achieve equilibrium between employer and employee goals and needs, HRM departments focus on these three general functions or activities: planning, implementation, and evaluation. The planning function refers to the development of human resource policies and regulations. Human resource managers attempt to determine future HRM activities and plan for the implementation of HRM procedures to help companies realize their goals.

Implementation of HRM plans involves four primary activities: acquisition, development, compensation, and maintenance. Acquisition entails the hiring of workers most likely to help a company attain its goals. The development function encompasses the training of workers to perform their tasks in accordance with company strategy.This activity also involves company efforts to control and change employee behavior via reviews, appraisals, incentives, and discipline. Compensation covers the payment of employees for their services. Maintenance requires structuring labor relationshe interaction between a company's management and its unionized employees and ensuring compliance with federal and state employment laws. Finally, the evaluation function includes the assessment of a company's HRM policies to determine whether they are effective.

HISTORY

Key principles and practices associated with HRM date back to the beginning of mankind. Mechanisms were developed for the selection of tribal leaders, for example, and knowledge was recorded and passed on to youth about safety, health, hunting, and gathering. More advanced HRM functions were developed as early as 1000 and 2000 B.C. Employee screening tests have been traced back to 1115 B.C. in China, for instance. And the earliest form of industrial education, the apprentice system, was started in ancient Greek and Babylonian civilizations before gaining prominence during medieval times. Since the inception of modem management theory, the terminology used to describe the role and function of workers has evolved from "personnel" to "industrial relations" to "employee relations" to "human resources." While all of these terms remain in use, "human resources" most accurately represents the view of workers by contemporary management theory: as valuable resources managed in the same manner as other valuable resources, according to the authors of Human Resource Management.

The need for an organized form of HRM emerged during the industrial revolution, as the manufacturing process evolved from a cottage system to factory production. As the United States shifted from an agricultural economy to an industrial economy, companies were forced to develop and implement effective ways of recruiting and keeping skilled workers. In addition, industrialization helped spur immigration, as the country opened its borders to fill industrial positions. Filling these jobs with immigrants, however, created an even greater need for adequate management of employees.

Between the 1880s and the 1940s, immigration rose significantly and remained robust until World War II. Advertisements circulated throughout the world depicting the United States as the land of opportunity where good-paying industrial jobs were plentiful. As a result, the country had a steady stream of low-skill, low-cost immigrant workers who occupied manufacturing, construction, and machinery operation positions. Even though these employees performed largely routine tasks, managers faced serious obstacles when trying to manage them since they spoke different languages. Early human resource management techniques included social welfare approaches aimed at helping immigrants adjust to their jobs and to life in the United States. These programs assisted immigrants in learning English and obtaining housing and medical care. In addition, these techniques promoted supervisory training in order to increase productivity.

While some companies paid attention to the "human" side of employment, however, others did not. Therefore, other factors such as hazardous working conditions and pressure from labor unions also increased the importance of effective management of human resources. Along with the manufacturing efficiencies brought about by industrialization came several shortcomings related to working conditions. These problems included: hazardous tasks, long hours, and unhealthy work environments. The direct cause of employers seeking better HRM programs was not poor working conditions, but rather the protests and pressures generated by workers and organized labor unions. Indeed, labor unions, which had existed as early as 1790 in the United States, became much more powerful during the late 1800s and early 1900s.

There were two other particularly important contributing factors to the origination of modem HRM during that period. The first was the industrial welfare movement, which represented a shift in the way that managers viewed employeesrom nonhuman resources to human beings. That movement resulted in the creation of medical care and educational facilities.

The second factor was Frederick W. Taylor's (1856-1915)Scientific Management, a landmark book that outlined management methods for attaining greater productivity from low-level production workers.

The first corporate employment department designed to address employee concerns was created by the B.F. Goodrich Company in 1900. In 1902 National Cash Register formed a similar department to handle worker grievances, wage administration, record keeping, and many other functions that would later be relegated to HRM departments at most large. U.S. companies. HRM as a professional discipline was especially bolstered by the passage of the Wagner Act in 1935 (also known as the National Labor Relations Act), which remained the basic U.S. labor law through the 1990s. It augmented the power of labor unions and increased the role and importance of personnel managers.

During the 1930s and 1940s the general focus of HRM changed from a focus on worker efficiency and skills to employee satisfaction. That shift became especially pronounced after World War II, when a shortage of skilled labor forced companies to pay more attention to workers' needs. Employers, influenced by the famous Hawthorne productivity studies and similar research, began to emphasize personal development and improved working conditions as a means of motivating employees.

In the 1960s and 1970s the federal government furthered the HRM movement with a battery of regulations created to enforce fair treatment of workers, such as the Equal Pay Act of 1963, the Civil Rights Act of 1964, the Employee Retirement Income Security Act of 1974 (ERISA), and the Occupational Safety and Health Act of 1970. Because of these acts, companies began placing greater emphasis on HRM in order to avoid lawsuits for violating this legislation. These regulations created an entirely new legal role for HRM professionals. Furthermore, during the 1970s, HRM gained status as a recognized profession with the advent of human resource programs in colleges. By the end of the 1970s, virtually all medium-sized and large companies and institutions had some type of HRM program in place to handle recruitment, training, regulatory compliance, dismissal, and other related issues. HRM's importance continued to grow during the 1980s for several reasons. Changing workforce values, for example, required the skills of HRM professionals to adapt organizational structures to a new generation of workers with different attitudes about authority and conformity. Shifting demographics forced changes in the way workers were hired, fired, and managed. Other factors contributing to the importance of HRM during the 1980s and 1990s were increasing education levels, growth of service and white-collar jobs, corporate restructuring (including reductions in middle management), more women in the workforce, slower domestic market growth, greater international competition, and new federal and state regulations.

THE FOCUS OF HRM

Businesses and organizations rely on three major resources: physical resources, such as materials and equipment; financial resources, including cash, credit, and debt; and human resources or workers. In its broadest sense, HRM refers to the management of all decisions within an organization that are related to people. In practice, however, HRM is a tool used to try to make optimum use of human resources, to foster individual development, and to comply with government mandates. Larger organizations typically have an HRM department and its primary objective is making company goals compatible with employee goals insofar as possible. Hence, for a company to attain its goals, it must have employees who will help it attain them.

Towards this end, R. Wayne Pace, writing in Human Resource Development, identifies seven underlying assumptions that provide a foundation and direction for HRM. First is the acknowledgment of individual worth, suggesting that companies recognize and value individual contributions. Second is that employees are resources who can learn new skills and ideas and can be trained to occupy new positions in the organization. Third is that quality of work life is a legitimate concern, and that employees have a right to safe, clean, and pleasant surroundings. A fourth assumption is the need for continuous learning; talents and skills must be continually refined in the long-term interests of the organization.

A fifth assumption supporting the existence of an organized HRM within a company or institution is that opportunities are constantly changing and companies need methods to facilitate continual worker adaptation. Sixth is employee satisfaction, which implies that humans have a right to be satisfied by their work and that employers have a responsibility and profit motivation to try to match a worker's skills with his or her job.

The seventh and final assumption is that HRM encompasses a much broader scope than technical trainingmployees need to know more than the requirements of a specific task in order to make their maximum contribution.

THE ROLE, POSITION, AND STRUCTURE OF HRM DEPARTMENTS

In Personnel Management, Paul S. Greenlaw and John P. Kohl describe three distinct, interrelated fields of interest addressed by the HRM discipline: human relations, organization theory, and decision areas. Human relations encompass matters such as individual motivation, leadership, and group relationships. Organization theory refers to job design, managerial control, and work flow through the organization. Decision areas encompass interests related to the acquisition, development, compensation, and maintenance of human resources.

Although the method and degree to which those areas of interest are handled vary among different HRM departments, a few general rules characterize the responsibilities, positioning, and structure of most HRM divisions.

HRM department responsibilities, other than related legal and clerical duties, can be classified by individual, organizational, and career areas. Individual management entails helping employees identify their strengths and weaknesses, correct their shortcomings, and then make their best contribution to the enterprise. These duties are carried out through a variety of activities such as performance reviews, training, and testing. Organizational development focuses on fostering a successful system that maximizes human, and other, resources. This important duty also includes the creation and maintenance of a change program, which allows the organization to respond to evolving outside and internal influences. The third responsibility, career development, involves matching individuals with the most suitable jobs and career paths.

The positioning of HRM departments is ideally near the theoretic organizational center, with maximum access to all divisions and management levels. In larger organizations the HRM function might be headed by a vice president, while smaller entities will have a middle-level manager as head of HRM. In any case, because the HRM department is charged with managing the productivity and development of workers at all levels, the top HRM manager ideally has access to, and the support of, key decision makers.

In addition, the HRM department should be situated in such a way that it has horizontal access, or is able to communicate effectively with all divisions within the company. Horizontal access allows HRM to integrate, educate, and train the workforce, and to facilitate changes that affect one division and indirectly influence other segments of the company or institution. The structure of HRM departments differs according to the type and size of the organization that they serve. But many large organizations (including governments, institutions, manufacturing companies, and service firms) organize HRM employee development functions around various clusters of worker shey conduct recruiting, administrative, and other duties in a central location. Different employee development groups for each department are necessary to train and develop employees in specialized areas, such as sales, engineering, marketing, or executive education. In contrast, some HRM departments are completely independent and are organized purely by function. The same training department, for example, serves all divisions of the organization.

HRM IMPLEMENTATION ACTIVITIES

To fulfill their basic role and achieve their goals, HRM professionals and departments engage in a variety of activities in order to execute their human resource plans. HRM implementation activities fall into four functional groups, each of which includes related legal responsibilities: acquisition, development, compensation, and maintenance.

ACQUISITION

Acquisition duties consist of human resource planning for employees, which includes activities related to analyzing employment needs, determining the necessary skills for positions, identifying job and industry trends, and forecasting future employment levels and skill requirements. These tasks may be accomplished using such tools and techniques as questionnaires, interviews, statistical analysis, building skill inventories, and designing career path charts. Four specific goals of effective human resource planning are:

1. Sustaining stable workforce levels during ups and downs in output, which can reduce unnecessary employment costs and liabilities and increase employee morale that would otherwise suffer in the event of lay-offs.

2. Preventing a high turnover rate among younger recruits.

3. Reducing problems associated with replacing key decision makers in the event of an unexpected absence.

4. Making it possible for financial resource managers to efficiently plan departmental budgets.

The acquisition function also encompasses activities related to recruiting workers, such as designing evaluation tests and interview methods. Ideally, the chief goal is to hire the most-qualified candidates without encroaching on federal regulations or allowing decision makers to be influenced by unrelated stereotypes. HRM departments at some companies may choose to administer honesty or personality tests, or to test potential candidates for drug use.

Recruitment responsibilities also include ensuring that the people in the organization are honest and adhere to strict government regulations pertaining to discrimination and privacy. To that end, human resource managers establish and document detailed recruiting and hiring procedures that protect applicants and diminish the risk of lawsuits.

DEVELOPMENT

The second major HRM function, human resource development, refers to performance appraisal and training activities. The basic goal of appraisal is to provide feedback to employees concerning their performance. This feedback allows them to evaluate the appropriateness of their behavior in the eyes of their coworkers and managers, correct weaknesses, and improve their contribution. HRM professionals must devise uniform appraisal standards, develop review techniques, train managers to administer the appraisals, and then evaluate and follow up on the effectiveness of performance reviews. They must also tie the appraisal process into compensation and incentive strategies, and work to ensure that federal regulations are observed. Training and development activities include the determination, design, execution, and analysis of educational programs. Orientation programs, for example, are usually necessary to acclimate new hires to the company. The HRM training and education role may encompass a wide variety of tasks, depending on the type and extent of different programs.

In any case, the HRM professional ideally is aware of the fundamentals of learning and motivation, and must carefully design effective training and development programs that benefit the overall organization as well as the individual. Training initiatives may include apprenticeship, internship, job rotation, mentoring, and new skills programs.

COMPENSATION

Compensation, the third major HRM function, refers to HRM duties related to paying employees and providing incentives for them. HRM professionals are typically charged with developing wage and salary systems that accomplish specific organizational objectives, such as employee retention, quality, satisfaction, and motivation. Ultimately, their aim is to establish wage and salary levels that maximize the company's investment in relation to its goals. This is often successfully accomplished with performance based incentives.

In particular, HRM managers must learn how to create compensation equity within the organization that doesn't hamper morale and that provides sufficient financial motivation. Besides financial compensation and fringe benefits, effective HRM managers also design programs that reward employees by meeting their emotional needs, such as recognition for good work.

MAINTENANCE

The fourth principal HRM function, maintenance of human resources, encompasses HRM activities related to employee benefits, safety and health, and worker-management relations. Employee benefits are non-incentive-oriented compensation, such as health insurance and free parking, and are often used to transfer non taxed compensation to employees. The three major categories of benefits managed by HRM managers are: employee services, such as purchasing plans, recreational activities, and legal services; vacations, holidays, and other allowed absences; and insurance, retirement, and health benefits. To successfully administer a benefits program, HRM professionals need to understand tax incentives, retirement investment plans, and purchasing power derived from a large base of employees.

Human resource maintenance activities related to safety and health usually entail compliance with federal laws that protect employees from hazards in the workplace. Regulations emanate from the federal Occupational Safety and Health Administration, for instance, and from state workers' compensation and federal Environmental Protection Agency laws. HRM managers must work to minimize the company's exposure to risk by implementing preventive safety and training programs.

They are also typically charged with designing detailed procedures to document and handle injuries. Maintenance tasks related to worker-management relations primarily entail: working with labor unions, handling grievances related to misconduct such as theft or sexual harassment, and devising systems to foster cooperation. Activities in this arena include contract negotiation, developing policies to accept and handle worker grievances, and administering programs to enhance communication and cooperation.

EVALUATION OF HRM METHODS

One of the most critical aspects of HRM is evaluating HRM methods and measuring their results. Even the most carefully planned and executed HRM programs are meaningless without some way to judge their effectiveness and confirm their credibility. The evaluation of HRM methods and programs should include both internal and external assessments. Internal evaluations focus on the costs versus the benefits of HRM methods, whereas external evaluations focus on the overall benefits of HRM methods in achieving company goals. Larger human resource departments often use detailed, advanced data gathering and statistical analysis techniques to test the success of their initiatives. The results can then be used to adjust HRM programs or even to make organizational changes.The authors of Human Resources Management posit four factors, the "four Cs," that should be used to determine whether or not an HRM department or individual program is succeeding: commitment, competence, cost-effectiveness, and congruence. In testing commitment, the HRM manager asks to what extent do policies enhance the commitment of people to the organization? Commitment is necessary to cultivate loyalty, improve performance, and optimize cooperation among individuals and groups.

Competence refers to the extent to which HRM policies attract, keep, and develop employees: Do HRM policies result in the right skills needed by the organization being available at the proper time and in the necessary quantity? Likewise, cost-effectiveness, the third factor, measures the fiscal proficiency of given policies in terms of wages, benefits, absenteeism, turnover, and labor/management disputes. Finally, analysis of congruence helps to determine how HRM policies create and maintain cooperation between different groups within and outside the organization, including different departments, employees and their families, and managers and subordinates.

In addition to advanced data gathering and analysis techniques, several simple observations can be made that provide insight into the general effectiveness of a company's human resources. For example, the ratio of managerial costs to worker costs indicates the efficiency of an organization's labor force. In general, lower managerial costs indicate a more empowered and effective workforce. Revenues and costs per employee, when compared to related industry norms, can provide insight into HRM effectiveness.

Furthermore, the average speed at which job vacancies are filled is an indicator of whether or not the organization has acquired the necessary talents and competencies. Other measures of HRM success include employee complaint and customer satisfaction statistics, health insurance and workers' compensation claims, and independent quality ratings. In addition, the number of significant innovations made each year, such as manufacturing or product breakthroughs, suggest HRM's success at fostering an environment that rewards new ideas and is amenable to change.

Besides evaluating these internal aspects of HRM programs, companies also must assess the effectiveness of HRM programs by their impact on overall business success. In other words, companies must link their evaluation of HRM methods with company performance to determine whether these methods are helping their business by increasing quality, reducing costs, expanding market share, and so forth. Ultimately, companies must make sure that they have the right amount of properly skilled employees performing tasks necessary for the attainment of company goals and that greater revenues and profits result from HRM efforts to increase the workforce and improve worker training and motivation.

LEGAL INFLUENCES

The field of HRM is greatly influenced and shaped by state and federal employment legislation, most of which is designed to protect workers from abuse by their employers. Indeed, one of the most important responsibilities of HRM professionals lies in compliance with regulations aimed at HRM departments.

The laws and court rulings can be categorized by their affect on the four primary HRM functional areas: acquisition, development, compensation, and maintenance.

The most important piece of HRM legislation, which affects all of the functional areas, is Title VII of the Civil Rights Act of 1964 and subsequent amendments, including the Civil

Rights Act of 1991. These acts made illegal the discrimination against employees or potential recruits for reasons of race, color, religion, sex, and national origin. It forces employers to achieve, and often document, fairness related to hiring, training, pay, benefits, and virtually all other activities and responsibilities related to HRM. The 1964 act established the Equal Employment Opportunity Commission (EEOC) to enforce the act, and provides for civil penalties in the event of discrimination. Possible penalties include forcing an organization to implement an affirmative action program to actively recruit and promote minorities that are underrepresented in a company's workforce or management.

The net result of the all encompassing civil rights acts is that HRM departments must carefully design and document numerous procedures to ensure compliance, or face potentially significant penalties.

In addition to the civil rights acts, a law affecting acquisition, or resource planning and selection, is the Equal Pay Act of 1963. This act forbids wage or salary discrimination based on sex, and mandates equal pay for equal work with few exceptions. Subsequent court rulings augmented the act by promoting the concept of comparable worth, or equal pay for unequal jobs of equal value or worth.

The important Age Discrimination in Employment Act of 1967, which was strengthened by amendments in the early 1990s, essentially protects workers 40 years of age and older from discrimination. The Fair Credit Reporting Act also affects acquisition activities, as employers who turn down applicants for credit reasons must provide the sources of the information that shaped their decision. Similarly, the Buckley Amendment of 1974 requires certain institutions to make records available to individuals and to receive permission before releasing those records to third parties.

The major laws affecting HRM development, or appraisal, training, and development, are the civil rights act, the equal pay act, and the age discrimination in employment act. All of those laws also affected the third HRM activity, rewards, or salary administration and incentive systems.

In addition, however, HRM reward programs must comply with a plethora of detailed legislation. The Davis-Bacon Act of 1931, for instance, requires the payment of minimum wages to nonfederal employees. The Walsh Healy Public Contracts Act of 1936 ensures that employees working as contractors for the federal government will be compensated fairly. Importantly, the Fair Labor Standards Act of 1938 mandates employer compliance with restrictions related to minimum wages, overtime provisions, child labor, and workplace safety. Other major laws affecting rewards include: the Tax Reform Acts of 1969, 1976, and 1986; the Economic Recovery Tax Act of 1981; the Revenue Act of 1978; and the Tax Equity and Fiscal Responsibility Act of 1982.

Perhaps the most regulated realm of the HRM field is maintenance (or benefits), safety and health, and employee/management relations. Chief among regulations in this arena is the Occupational Safety and Health Act of 1970, which established the Occupational Safety and Health Administration. That act was designed to force employers to provide safe and healthy work environments and to make organizations liable for workers' safety. The sweeping act has ballooned to include thousands of regulations backed by civil and criminal penalties, including jail time and fines for company executives. Also of import are state workers' compensation laws, which require employers to make provisions to pay for work-related injuries, and forces HRM managers to create and document safety procedures and programs that reduce a company's liability.

The Wagner Act of 1935 is the main piece of legislation governing union/management relations, and is a chief source of regulation for HRM departments. Other important laws related to HRM maintenance include: the Norris-Laguardia Act of 1932, the Social Security Act of 1935, the Taft-Hartley Act of 1947, and the Landrum-Griffin Act of 1959.

FORCES CHANGING HRM

In the 1990s several forces were shaping the broad field of HRM. The first key force, new technologiesarticularly information technologyrought about the decentralization of communications and the shake-up of existing paradigms of human interaction and organizational theory. Satellite communications, computers and networking systems, fax machines, and other devices were facilitating rapid change. Moreover, since these technologies helped blur the lines between work time and personal time by enabling employees to work at home, HRM professionals began adopting "management by objective" approaches to human resources instead of the traditional "management by sight" method. A second important change affecting HRM was new organizational structures that began to emerge during the 1980s and continued through the 1990s. Because many companies began expanding their operations and diversifying their products and services, the central decision-making system failed to respond quickly enough to managers' needs and concerns.

Therefore, companies started scrapping traditional, hierarchical organizational structures in favor of flatter, decentralized management systems. Consequently, fewer managers were involved in the decision-making process and companies were adopting more of a team approach to management. HRM professionals, as the agents of change, were charged with reorganizing workers and increasing their efficiency. These efforts also resulted in the proliferation of part-time, or contract, employees, which required human resource strategies that contrasted with those applicable to full time workers.

A third change factor was accelerating market globalization, which was increasing competition and demanding greater performance out of workers, often at diminished levels of compensation. To compete abroad, companies were looking to their HRM professionals to augment initiatives related to quality, productivity, and innovation.

Other factors changing HRM include: an accelerating rate of change and turbulence, resulting in higher employee turnover and the need for more responsive, open-minded workers; rapidly changing demographics; and increasing income disparity as the demand for highly educated workers increases at the expense of lower-wage employees.

CHAPTER – 2
Scope of Human Resource Management

HRM in Personnel Management:

This is typically direct manpower management that involves manpower planning, hiring (recruitment and selection), training and development, induction and orientation, transfer, promotion, compensation, layoff and retrenchment, employee productivity. The overall objective here is to ascertain individual growth, development and effectiveness which indirectly contribute to organizational development.

It also includes performance appraisal, developing new skills, disbursement of wages, incentives, allowances, traveling policies and procedures and other related courses of actions.

HRM in Employee Welfare: This particular aspect of HRM deals with working conditions and amenities at workplace. This includes a wide array of responsibilities and services such as safety services, health services, welfare funds, social security and medical services. It also covers appointment of safety officers, making the environment worth working, eliminating workplace hazards, support by top management, job safety, safeguarding machinery, cleanliness, proper ventilation and lighting, sanitation, medical care, sickness benefits, employment injury benefits, personal injury benefits, maternity benefits, unemployment benefits and family benefits.

It also relates to supervision, employee counseling, establishing harmonious relationships with employees, education and training. Employee welfare is about determining employees' real needs and fulfilling them with active participation of both management and employees.

In addition to this, it also takes care of canteen facilities, crèches, rest and lunch rooms, housing, transport, medical assistance, education, health and safety, recreation facilities, etc. HRM in Industrial Relations: Since it is a highly sensitive area, it needs careful interactions with labor or employee unions, addressing their grievances and settling the disputes effectively in order to maintain peace and harmony in the organization. It is the art and science of understanding the employment (union-management) relations, joint consultation, disciplinary procedures, solving problems with mutual efforts, understanding human behavior and maintaining work relations, collective bargaining and settlement of disputes.

The main aim is to safeguarding the interest of employees by securing the highest level of understanding to the extent that does not leave a negative impact on organization. It is about establishing, growing and promoting industrial democracy to safeguard the interests of both employees and management.

The scope of HRM is extremely wide, thus, cannot be written concisely. However, for the sake of convenience and developing understanding about the subject, we divide it in three categories mentioned above.

Staffing Role of the HR Manager: Strategic Workforce Planning

Strategies to Deal with Shortage of Talent during the Boom Years. The way to deal with such a situation was to ensure that the number of people being taken in was based on current and future demand scenarios and identify gaps and surpluses in key skill sets. For instance, in the US, the shortage of those with Java skills was so huge that anyone with an elementary knowledge of the skill was immediately taken in the companies. This meant that the HR unit was simply filling up positions without any strategic planning. Hence, many organizations realized that hiring people without the requisite skills just to fill up positions would do more harm than good to the companies and hence, a conscious decision was taken by the HR managers in conjunction with the line managers to have forecasts of how many employees they would need over a quarter.

The point here is that the constant bickering between the HR managers and the line managers took a toll on organizational efficiency and hence, this compromise was arrived at wherein the demand for specific skill sets had to be forecasted by the line managers and the HR managers would then deal with hiring accordingly. The third aspect of the staffing and hiring activity is that many HR managers during the boom years advised the line managers to find employees from other divisions who wanted a change in their job profiles and roles. This internal filling up of positions by inter-division and intra company movement was effective in many companies like Fidelity. Further, overtime by key resources and hiring temporary workers were the norm in many companies. Of course, the overtime work was adequately compensated and employees who were doing so were given additional benefits. Staffing Strategies during the Ongoing Recession With the boom years over, the HR managers in recent years are breathing easy as they no longer have to run around trying to meet recruitment targets. Of course, the current challenge before the HR managers to manage the downturn and smoothen the downsizing underway in many organizations. To ensure these objectives in these economically harsh times, HR managers are resorting to passive measures as the first line of action wherein they indicate to the employees that they are on PIP or Performance Improvement Plans and this usually results in natural attrition.

Next, instead of downsizing, the HR managers are reducing recruitment so that they do not have to fire employees and instead, these employees can be accommodated elsewhere in the organization. These are some of the aspects of the strategic workplace planning within the hiring and staffing activity that some respected companies follow.

Role of Human Resource Management (HRM) in Leadership Development

Leadership Development in Successful Companies

The previous articles have discussed how the HRM function is now seen as a critical and crucial component of the organizational support functions. In particular, we have analyzed how effective people management goes a long way in ensuring better economic performance. Among the components of people, management that the HRM function does is the aspect related to leadership development. Research into the HRM practices of successful companies has shown that these companies significantly outperform their peers in terms of economic profitability by following the leadership development practices discussed in this article. By successful companies, we mean those companies in the Fortune 100 list that have managed to retain their position in the firms over a decade. To put this in perspective, it needs to be remembered that many companies that were in the Fortune 100 list for a few years failed to retain their positions in subsequent years and hence, the fact that these companies have managed to stay in the hunt means that they have outperformed their peers and competitors.

The Components of Leadership Development

The leadership development programs in these companies follow the philosophy of grounding them in value, the expected contributions from the leaders are defined, and the organizational culture geared towards inspiring leaders. Next, the performance management system in these companies is tied to the company's business strategy and it includes talent development activities and leadership objectives that are articulated clearly and succinctly. In other words, promotions are based on individual performance as well as people development activities and these in turn are linked to the business strategy and objectives. These companies also have a leadership pipeline, which means that the leadership development is embedded in their strategic workforce planning which is comprehensive, and longer term oriented.

These companies also ensure that they divide their workforce into job families and the potential leaders are identified and groomed for higher roles and responsibilities. In many of these companies, it is common to find lists of potential leaders known as high potentials who are earmarked for fast track career progression based on the organizational assessment of the skills and capabilities of these leaders.

Further, the recruitment and training of new employees is based on longer-term analysis of demand and supply patterns, which ensure that newer generation of leaders, are hired into the company to replace those who have made it to the higher levels. Collaboration between the HRM Function and Senior Management. The HRM functions in these companies work on a collaborative model with their potential leaders which means that the job of people development is not left to the HRM function or the leaders alone. Instead, the potential leaders are identified and then their performance is linked to the enabling and empowerment of others to move up the chain. In other words, the ability to spot talent and identify leaders for the future is done by both the HRM function and the senior management who work in tandem in this effort. Research into these successful companies has shown that the people management in these companies is world class and the contributing factor that differentiates these companies from others is that the HRM function plays a critical role throughout the employee lifecycle and not at the recruitment and training phase alone. The other factor is that the leaders in these companies are expected to have skill sets that match the need for adapting to the challenges of the 21st century business landscape. In other words, these companies groom the leaders of the future right from the middle management level.

Closing Thoughts

Finally, leadership is a combination of natural abilities and the organizational nurturing of the employees with those skills. Hence, this interplay between nature and nurture is what determines the success or otherwise of the HRM function and the senior management efforts to develop leadership in these companies.

Performance Management as a HR Management concept

There are different rounds to the appraisal process.

In the first round, the people who participate in an employee's appraisal are the employee and his or her manager. In this round, the manager gives a frank assessment of the employee's performance after giving a chance to the employee to self-assess. The second round consists of the manager and the manager's manager. This round is mostly about deciding the band in which the employee falls post the rating and in comparison with his or her peers. This process of rationalizing the employee's performance with others is called "normalization". In some organizations, this takes place in the third round where the HR manager is involved as well. In any case, the ratings cannot be decided without the HR manager's assent to the same. Once these rounds are over, the bonus level or the salary hike are decided.

What we have described in the above paragraphs is the way the system "ought" to work. However, as any HR professional or Industry magazines would tell you, the performance management process as it exists in many organizations leaves a lot to be desired. In fact, surveys and studies have found that the majority of employee's who quit organizations do so because of differences over their ratings. In other words, attrition is in many cases a direct consequence of the way in which the performance management process is managed.

The question as to why this happens can be best understood if we understand the dynamics inherent in the process. For instance, despite exhortations from HR professionals and experts about letting personal biases and prejudices affect the process, in many cases, if the manager and the employee do not see eye to eye on many issues, the appraisal and the ratings are the place where this difference of opinion comes out into the open.

Further, the organizations are themselves to blame in some cases as the process of "normalization" means a "winner takes all" approach which leaves the moderate performers bracketed with the poor performers. The point here is not to belittle the competitive environment that is the reason for this. On the other contrary, what is needed is a more holistic approach towards performance management that takes into account the varying needs of employee's and a broader appreciation of differing working styles and motivations.

HR Challenges - How to cope with them efficiently ?

Human Resource Management used to be considered as other conventional administrative jobs. But over a period of time, it has evolved as a strategic function to improve working environment, plan out human resources needs and strike a balance between the organization and employers in order to increase organizational productivity and meet organizational goals. Not to exaggerate but in today's highly competitive world it has gradually become one of the most important functions of an organization.

It is really a huge challenge to understand the psychology of workforce, retain the best talents of the industry, motivate them to perform better and handle diversity while maintaining unity simultaneously, especially in countries like India, where it is still evolving. Globalization has resulted in many positive developments but it has left many concerns for HR managers.

In today's tough world and tight job market, coordinating a

multicultural or diverse workforce is a real challenge for HR department.

To remain in business, human resource managers need to efficiently address following human resource challenges:

> **Handling Multicultural / Diverse Workforce:** Dealing with people from different age, gender, race, ethnicity, educational background, location, income, parental status, religious beliefs, marital status and ancestry and work experience can be a challenging task for HR managers. With this, managing people with different set of ideologies, views, lifestyles and psychology can be very risky. Effective communication, adaptability, agility and positive attitude of HR managers can bind the diverse workforce and retain talents in the organization.

> **Managing Change:** Who wants to change their ideology or way of working? Neither you nor I. How can we expect others to change then? Bringing change in organizational processes and procedures, implementing it and then managing it is one of the biggest concerns of HR managers. Business environment is so volatile. Technology keeps changing every now and then. All thanks to globalization. Upgrading the existing technology and training people for them is a real headache for HR department. The success rate of technology change depends how well HRD can handle the change and manage people issues in the process.

- ➢ **Retaining the Talents:** Globalization has given freedom to working professionals to work anywhere in the world. Now that they have endless lucrative opportunities to work, hiring and retaining the best industry talent is no joke. Maintaining harmonious relations with them, providing excellent work environment and offering more remuneration and perks than your competitors can retain and motivate them.

- ➢ **Conflict Management:** HR managers should know how to handle employee-employer and employee-employee conflicts without hurting their feelings. Although it is almost impossible to avoid conflicts among people still handling them tactfully can help HR managers to resolve the issues. They should be able to listen to each party, decide and communicate to them in a convincing manner in order to avoid future conflicts.

HR professional must be proactive with all strategies and action plans in order to meet the changing needs of the organization. They must be thorough with the basic functions of HR including planning, organizing, leading and controlling human resources

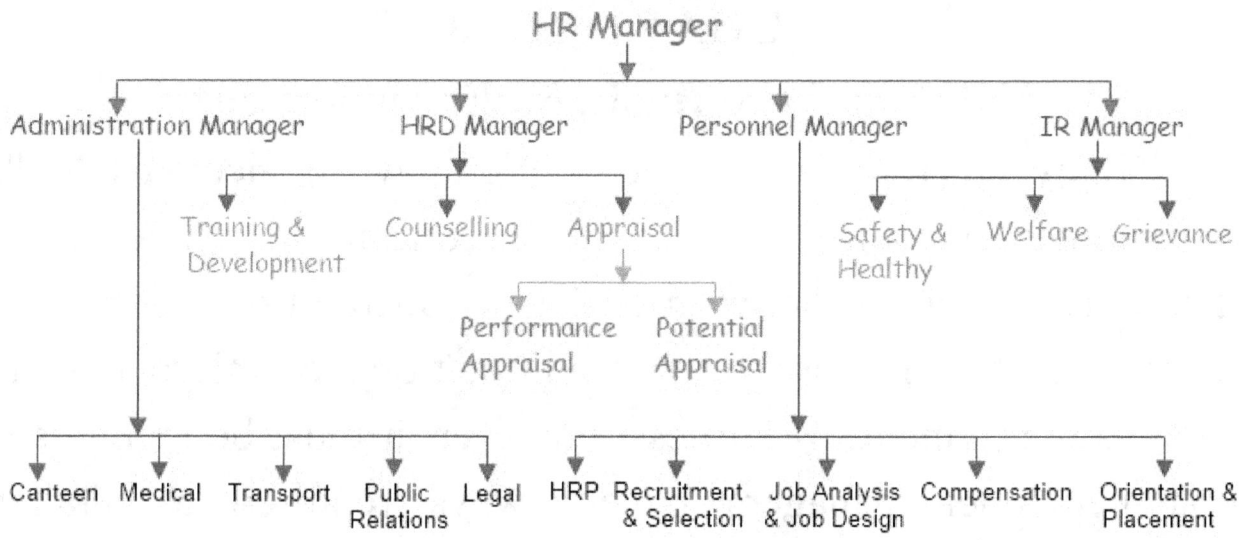

www.whatishumanresource.com

CHAPTER – 3
HRM and the Business Environment

Many practitioners and academics have neglected HRM's environmental context, preferring to concentrate on technical detail. This is consistent with criticisms of traditional personnel management for its narrow focus on functional or 'micro' matters such as recruitment. In fairness, however, it must be recognised that personnel managers have always required a detailed knowledge of employment legislation, together with an understanding of industrial tribunals and trade union organization. Nevertheless, this represents a restricted selection from the wide range of environmental factors impacting on people management.

Often exponents of HRM have been no better than traditional personnel managers in this respect. Kochan and Dyer (1995: 343) argue that despite the obsession with strategy, HRM theories have a fundamental weakness: 'a myopic viewpoint which fails to look beyond the boundary of the firm'. Without the ability or the interest to locate their activities in a wider environmental setting, human resource practitioners can lose contact with the 'bleeding edge' of organizational survival. To counter short-sightedness and parochialism, HR managers must widen their perspectives beyond their own organizations (Beardwell and Holden, 1994: 613). In contrast to colleagues in marketing, production and finance, people managers seem less prepared to function in a competitive world.

This chapter addresses this wider perspective and introduces a number of fundamental issues which are developed further in later chapters, for example:

> ➤ What is the connection between education and skill levels and national success?

> ➤ To what extent is the nature of people management determined by prevailing political ideology and national culture?

> ➤ Is HRM simply a managerial reaction to the spread of market economies throughout the world?

> ➤ Is there a contradiction between HRM's long-term emphasis and the short-term priorities of the stock market?

We observed in the previous chapter that the essence of HRM lies in the competitive advantage to be gained from making the most of an organization's human resources. However, it is obvious that we are constrained by the availability of suitable people - a factor which is heavily dependent on environmental variables. As we shall see, they include:

- the implications of world and national economic conditions for business growth
- the effect of inflation on the perceived value of wages;
- the traditions of local business culture;
- the particular nature of national employment markets.

In effect, therefore, these variables have a 'macro' effect on the utilization of human resources. Additionally, in this chapter we consider other effects caused by the activities of external stakeholders, such as:

- competitors' utilization and demand for human resources;
- multinational organizations and strategic alliances leading to restructuring or integration on a global basis;
- economic and legislative actions by governments;
- resistance or cooperation from trade unions;
- pressure on senior managers to cut costs and maximise shareholder value. We begin the chapter with an examination of situational factors at the international and national levels.

Nature of Human Resource Management

Human Resource Management brings organizations and people together so that the goals of each are met. The nature of HRM includes:

Broader function

Human Resource Management is a comprehensive function because it is about managing people in the organization. It covers all types of people in the organization from workers till the top level management.

People oriented

Human resource is the core of all the processes of human resource management. So HRM is the process which brings people and organizations together so that their goals can be achieved.

Action oriented

Human resource management believes in taking actions in

order to achieve individual and organizational goals rather than just keeping records and procedures.

Development oriented

Development of employees is an essential function of human resource management in order to get maximum satisfaction from their work so that they give their best to the organization.

Continuous function

As human resource is a living factor among all factors of production therefore it requires continuous improvement and innovations in order to get excellence. So it requires a constant alertness and awareness of human relations and there importance in every day to day operations.

Future oriented

HRM is very important activity which helps organization to achieve its objectives in future by providing well motivated and competent employees.

Nature and scope of Human Resource Management (HRM)

Nature of HRM:

1. HRM involves management functions like planning, organizing, directing and controlling.
2. It involves procurement, development, maintenance and management of human resource.
3. It helps to achieve individual, organizational and social objectives.
5. HRM is a mighty disciplinary subject. It includes the

study of management psychology communication, economics and sociology.

5. It involves team spirit and team work.

The scope of HRM refers to all the activities that come under the banner of HRM. The activities are as follows

1. **Human resources planning:** - Human resource planning is a process by which the company to identify the number of jobs vacant, whether the company has excess staff or shortage of staff and to deal with this excess or shortage.

2. **Job analysis design:** - Another important area of HRM is job analysis. Job analysis gives a detailed explanation about each and every job in the company. Based on this job analysis the company prepares advertisements.

3. **Recruitment and selection:** - Based on information collected from job analysis the company prepares advertisements and publishes them in the news papers. A number of applications are received after the advertisement is published, interviews are conducted and the right employee is selected thus recruitment and selection are yet another important areas of HRM.

4. **Orientation and induction:** - Once the employees have been selected an induction or orientation program is conducted. The employees are informed about the background of the company. They are told about the organizational culture and values and work ethics and introduce to the other employees.

5. **Training and development:** - Every employee goes under training program which helps him to put up a better performance on the job. Training program is also conducted for existing staff that have a lot of experience. This is called refresher training. Training and development is one area were the company spends a huge amount.

6. **Performance appraisal:** - Once the employee has put in around 1 year of service, performance appraisal is conducted i.e. the HR department checks the performance of the employee. Based on these appraisal future promotions, incentives, increments in salary are decided.

7. **Compensation planning and remuneration:** - There are various rules regarding compensation and other benefits. It is the job of the HR department to look into remuneration and compensation planning.

8. **Motivation, welfare, health and safety:** - Motivation becomes important to sustain the number of employees in the company. It is the job of the HR department to look into the different methods of motivation. Apart from this certain health and safety regulations have to be followed for the benefits of the employees.

9. **Industrial relations:** - Another important area of HRM is maintaining co-ordinal relations with the union members. This will help the organization to prevent strikes lockouts and ensure smooth working in the company.

Nature and scope of HRM

Human resources may be defined as the total knowledge, skills, creative abilities, talents and aptitudes of an organization's workforce, as well as the values, attitudes, approaches and beliefs of the individuals involved in the affairs of the organization. It is the sum total or aggregate of inherent abilities, acquired knowledge and skills represented by the talents and aptitudes of the persons employed in the organization.

The human resources are multidimensional in nature. From the national point of view, human resources may be defined as the knowledge, skills, creative abilities, talents and aptitudes obtained in the population; whereas from the viewpoint of the individual enterprise, they represent the total of the inherent abilities, acquired knowledge and skills as exemplified in the talents and aptitudes of its employees.

HumanResourceManagement:Nature

Human Resource Management is a process of bringing people and organizations together so that the goals of each are met.The various features of HRM include:

It is pervasive in nature as it is present in all enterprises. Its focus is on results rather than on rules. It tries to help employees develop their potential fully. It encourages employees to give their best to the organization. It is all about people at work, both as individuals and groups.

It tries to put people on assigned jobs in order to produce good results.

It helps an organization meet its goals in the future by providing for competent and well-motivated employees. It tries to build and maintain cordial relations between people working at various levels in the organization. It is a multi-disciplinary activity, utilizing knowledge and inputs drawn from psychology, economics, etc.

Human Resource Management:

Scope

The scope of HRM is very wide:

Personnel aspect-This is concerned with manpower planning, recruitment, selection, placement, transfer, promotion, training and development, layoff and retrenchment, remuneration, incentives, productivity etc.

Welfare aspect-It deals with working conditions and amenities such as canteens, creches, rest and lunch rooms, housing, transport, medical assistance, education, health and safety, recreation facilities, etc. Industrial relations aspect-This covers union-management relations, joint consultation, collective bargaining, grievance and disciplinary procedures, settlement of disputes, etc.

Human Resource Management: Objectives

To help the organization reach its goals. To ensure effective utilization and maximum development of human resources.

To ensure respect for human beings. To identify and satisfy the needs of individuals.

To ensure reconciliation of individual goals with those of the organization.

To achieve and maintain high morale among employees. To provide the organization with well-trained and well-motivated employees.

To increase to the fullest the employee's job satisfaction and self-actualization.

To develop and maintain a quality of work life. To be ethically and socially responsive to the needs of society. To develop overall personality of each employee in its multi-dimensional aspect.

To enhance employee's capabilities to perform the present job.

To equip the employees with precision and clarity in transaction of business.

To inculcate the sense of team spirit, team work and inter-team collaboration.

Human Resource Management: Functions

In order to achieve the above objectives, Human Resource Management undertakes the following activities:

Human resource or manpower planning.

Recruitment, selection and placement of personnel.

Training and development of employees.

Appraisal of performance of employees.

Taking corrective steps such as transfer from one job to another.

Remuneration of employees.

Social security and welfare of employees.

Setting general and specific management policy for organizational relationship.

Collective bargaining, contract negotiation and grievance handling.

Staffing the organization.

Aiding in the self-development of employees at all levels.

Developing and maintaining motivation for workers by providing incentives.

Reviewing and auditing manpower management in the organization

Potential Appraisal. Feedback Counseling.

Role Analysis for job occupants.

Job Rotation.

Quality Circle, Organization development and Quality of Working Life.

CHAPTER – 4
HUMAN RESOUCE PLANNING

Strategic HR Planning Skills

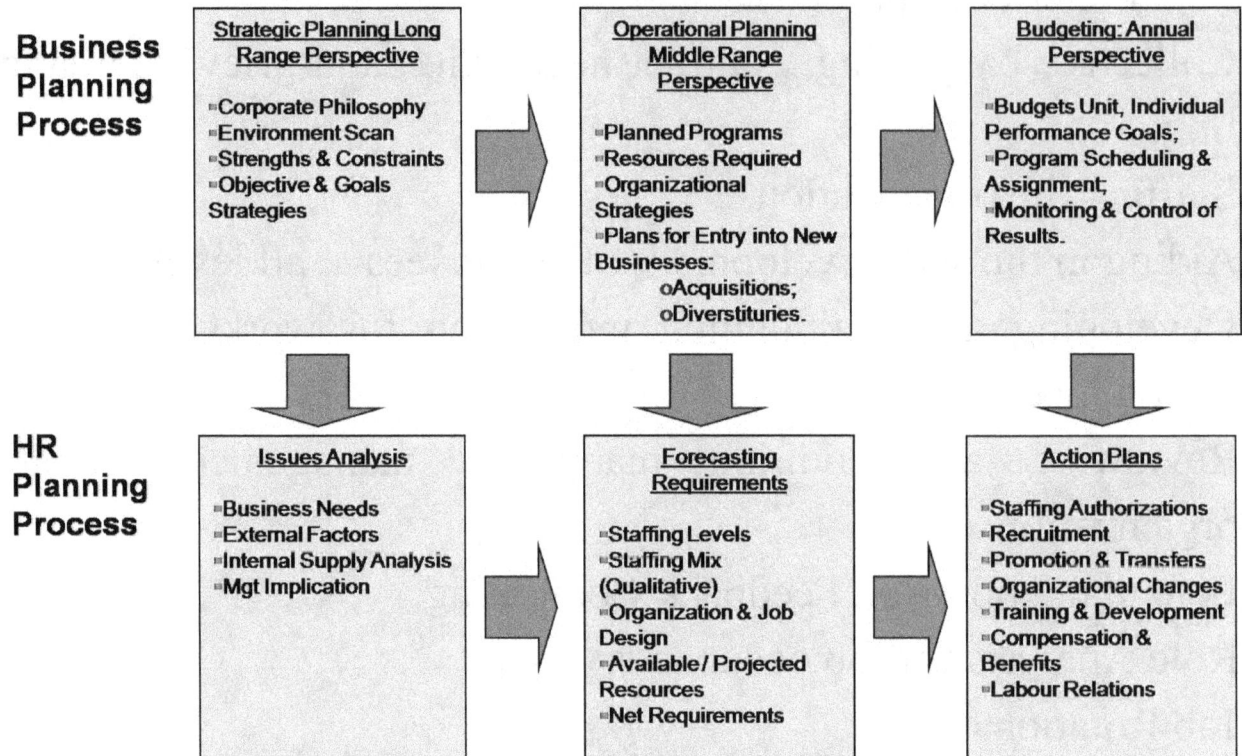

Human Resource Planning: an Introduction

A British Foreign Office official looking back over a career spanning the first half of the twentieth century commented: 'Year after year the fretters and worriers would come to me with their awful predictions of the outbreak of war. I denied it each time. I was only wrong twice!'Some would see this as the arrogant complacency to be associated with planners. Critics think of the inaccuracy and over-optimism of forecasting — the 'hockey stick' business growth projections. They regard planning as too inflexible, slow to respond to change, too conservative in assumptions and risk averse. These points are made about any sort of planning.

Practical benefits

When it concerns human resources, there are the more specific criticisms that it is over-quantitative and neglects the qualitative aspects of contribution. The issue has become not how many people should be employed, but ensuring that all members of staff are making an effective contribution. And for the future, the questions are what are the skills that will be required, and how will they be acquired.

There are others, though, that still regard the quantitative planning of resources as important. They do not see its value in trying to predict events, be they wars or takeovers. Rather, they believe there is a benefit from using planning to challenge assumptions about the future, to stimulate thinking.

For some there is, moreover, an implicit or explicit wish to get better integration of decision making and resourcing across the whole organisation, or greater influence by the centre over devolved operating units. Cynics would say this is all very well, but the assertion of corporate control has been tried and rejected. And is it not the talk of the process benefits to be derived self indulgent nonsense? Can we really afford this kind of intellectual dilettantism? Whether these criticisms are fair or not, supporters of human resource planning point to its practical benefits in optimising the use of resources and identifying ways of making them more flexible. For some organisations, the need to acquire and grow skills which take time to develop is paramount. If they fail to identify the business demand, both numerically and in the skills required, and secure the appropriate supply, then the capacity of the organisation to fulfil its function will be endangered.

Why human resource planning?

Human Resource Planning: an Introduction was written to draw these issues to the attention of HR or line managers. We address such questions as:

> what is human resource planning?
> how do organisations undertake this sort of exercise?
> what specific uses does it have?

In dealing with the last point we need to be able to say to hard pressed managers: why spend time on this activity rather than the other issues bulging your in tray? The report tries to meet this need by illustrating how human resource planning techniques can be applied to four key problems. It then concludes by considering the circumstances is which human resourcing can be used.

1. Determining the numbers to be employed at a new location

If organisations overdo the size of their workforce it will carry surplus or underutilised staff. Alternatively, if the opposite misjudgement is made, staff may be overstretched, making it hard or impossible to meet production or service deadlines at the quality level expected. So the questions we ask are:

> How can output be improved your through understanding the interrelation between productivity, work organisation and technological development? What does this mean for staff numbers?

> What techniques can be used to establish workforce requirements?

> Have more flexible work arrangements been considered?

> How are the staff you need to be acquired?

The principles can be applied to any exercise to define workforce requirements, whether it be a business start-up, a relocation, or the opening of new factory or office.

2. Retaining your highly skilled staff

Issues about retention may not have been to the fore in recent years, but all it needs is for organisations to lose key staff to realise that an understanding of the pattern of resignation is needed. Thus organisations should:

> monitor the extent of resignation

> discover the reasons for it

> establish what it is costing the organisation

> compare loss rates with other similar organisations.

Without this understanding, management may be unaware of how many good quality staff are being lost. This will cost the organisation directly through the bill for separation, recruitment and induction, but also through a loss of long-term capability.

Having understood the nature and extent of resignation steps can be taken to rectify the situation. These may be relatively cheap and simple solutions once the reasons for the departure of employees have been identified. But it will depend on whether the problem is peculiar to your own organisation, and whether it is concentrated in particular groups (eg by age, gender, grade or skill).

3. Managing an effective downsizing programme

This is an all too common issue for managers. How is the workforce to be cut painlessly, while at the same time protecting the long-term interests of the organisation? A question made all the harder by the time pressures management is under, both because of business necessities and employee anxieties. HRP helps by considering:

> the sort of workforce envisaged at the end of the exercise
> the pros and cons of the different routes to get there
> how the nature and extent of wastage will change during the run-down
> the utility of retraining, redeployment and transfers
> what the appropriate recruitment levels might be.

Such an analysis can be presented to senior managers so that the cost benefit of various methods of reduction can be assessed, and the time taken to meet targets established.

If instead the CEO announces on day one that there will be no compulsory redundancies and voluntary severance is open to all staff, the danger is that an unbalanced workforce will result, reflecting the take-up of the severance offer. It is often difficult and expensive to replace lost quality and experience.

4. Where will the next generation of managers come from?

Many senior managers are troubled by this issue. They have seen traditional career paths disappear. They have had to bring in senior staff from elsewhere. But they recognise that while this may have dealt with a short-term skills shortage, it has not solved the longer term question of managerial supply: what sort, how many, and where will they come from? To address these questions you need to understand:

- the present career system (including patterns of promotion and movement, of recruitment and wastage)
- the characteristics of those who currently occupy senior positions
- the organisation's future supply of talent.

This then can be compared with future requirements, in number and type. These will of course be affected by internal structural changes and external business or political changes. Comparing your current supply to this revised demand will show surpluses and shortages which will allow you to take corrective action such as:

- recruiting to meet a shortage of those with senior management potential
- allowing faster promotion to fill immediate gaps
- developing cross functional transfers for high fliers
- hiring on fixed-term contracts to meet short-term skills/experience deficits

> reducing staff numbers to remove blockages or forthcoming surpluses.

Thus appropriate recruitment, deployment and severance policies can be pursued to meet business needs. Otherwise processes are likely to be haphazard and inconsistent. The wrong sort of staff are engaged at the wrong time on the wrong contract. It is expensive and embarrassing to put such matters right.

How can HRP be applied?

The report details the sort of approach companies might wish to take. Most organisations are likely to want HRP systems:

> which are responsive to change
> where assumptions can easily be modified
> that recognise organisational fluidity around skills
> that allow flexibility in supply to be included
> that are simple to understand and use
> which are not too time demanding.

To operate such systems organisations need:

> appropriate demand models
> good monitoring and corrective action processes
> comprehensive data about current employees and the external labour market

an understanding how resourcing works in the organisation.

Human resource Planning Presentation

1. HUMAN RESOURCE PLANNING :

Human Resource Planning could be expressed as a process by which the management ensures the right number of people and right kind of people, at the right place, at the right time doing the right things for which they are recruited and placed for the achievement of goals of the organization. Human Resource may be regarded as the quantitative and qualitative measurement of workforce required in an organization. Human Resource Planning aims at the continuous supply of right kind of personnel to fill various positions in the organization. Human Resource Planning is a continuous process. In the words of Colman , "Manpower planning is the process of determining manpower requirements and the means of meeting those requirements in order to carryout the integrated plan of the organization".

2. HUMAN RESOURCE PLANNING :

According to Geister, "Manpower Planning is the process including forecasting, developing and controlling by which a firm ensures that it has the right number of people and the right kind of people at the right places, at the right time doing work for which they are economically most useful. Therefore, manpower planning consists of projecting future manpower requirements and developing manpower plans for the implementation of projections".

According to Dale S. Beach, "Human Resource Planning is a process of determining and assuring that the organization will have an adequate number of qualified persons, available at the proper times, performing jobs which meet the needs of the enterprise and which provide satisfaction for the individuals involved. Human Resource planning can not be rigid or static. It is amenable to modifications, review and adjustments in accordance with the needs of the organization or the changing circumstances

3. OBJECTIVES OF HRP :

i) ensure optimum use of human resources currently employed; ii) avoid imbalances in the distribution and allocation of human resources; iii) assess or forecast future skill requirements of the organization's overall objectives; iv) provide control measure to ensure availability of necessary resources when required; v) control the aspect of human resources; vi) formulate transfer and promotion policies

4. NATURE OF HRP :

The following points emerges after the analysis of various definitions : HRP presents an inventory of existing manpower of the organisation. Analysis of this resource helps in ascertaining the status of the available personnel and to discover untapped talent presently available with the organisation. HRP helps in determining the shortfall or surplus of the resource by comparing the total resource needs with the present supply. It also helps in projecting future HR needs. HRP is concerned with the initiation of various organisation progammes depending upon the demand and supply of human resources. Effective manpower planning must encompass the acquisition, utilization, improvement and preservation of the organisation's human resources. HR planning aim at ascertaining the manpower needs of the organisation both in number and kind.

5. SCOPE OF HRP :

1) Listing or current human resources 2) Assessing the context to which the current manpower is utilized to the advantage of the organizing. 3) Planning out the surplus human resource, if any, 4) Analyzing the requirements of manpower in future in the light of expansion plans, retirement of personnel etc. 5) Making human resource forecast 6) Designing training programme for different categories of human resource.

6. NEED FOR HRP :

HRP helps in proper recruitment and selection so that right type of people are available to man various positions in the organization. HRP also facilitates designing of training programmes for the employees to develop the required skills in them. HRP provides lead time for procuring personnel as the lead time given is a time-consuming process.

7. BENEFITS OF HRP :

HRP is an integral part of HRM and it helps in the following ways : HRP results in reduced labour costs as it helps the management to anticipate shortages and/or surpluses or HR, and correct these imbalances before they become unmanageable and expensive. HRP is the scientific way for planning employee development that is designed to make optimum use of workers' skills within the organization.

HRP enables identification of the gaps of the existing HR so that corrective training could be imparted. HRP leads of improvement in the overall "Business Planning" process. HRP helps in formulating managerial succession plan as a part of the replacement planning process. HRP leads to a greater awareness of the importance of sound manpower management throughout the organization HRP serves as a tool to evaluate the effect of alternative manpower actions and policies.

8. HRP at different levels :

HRP may broadly be carried out at Corporate, divisional and plant levels. It is better for HRP to start at the lowest level and them move upward. If personnel lower down in the organization start the following process, the organization shall reach the benefits of thinking of persons who are more familiar with the day to day problems. HRP at the plant level can be inducted by an operating committee on the basis of past data and future projections. The committee would formulate a manpower plan for the rest years. Planning would also include the number of employees required and the sources which could be utilized to meet these requirements.

At this level, HRP would also determine the number of promo table employees for the annual HR plan. At the end, the committee will evaluate the plans in the light of expected changes of all kinds within the next five years with the help of

HRP experts. Each department will have the divisional/departmental committee which would review the HR plans submitted by all the divisions in the plant. The divisional committee would integrate all the HR plans of which in turn would be submitted to the top management.

The Committee of top executives will review the plan submitted by the divisional committees and will develop similar plans for the headquarter staff. It will make projections of HR requirements of various kinds during the next five years. After the HR planning has been done at the top level, taking into consideration records regarding employee turnover due to death, retirement, resignations, terminations and absenteeism also, it will be integrated with the other organizational plans.

9. HRP PROCESS :

The process of HRP involves the following steps :
1. Determination of HRP objectives of HR planning
2. Current HR inventory 3. Demand Forecasting 4. Job requirements 5. Employment plan 6. Training and Development programme

10. HR planning is a continuous planning Objectives of HRP Appraisal of HRP Fig. The Human Resource Planning Process   Inventory of HR Skills(finding gap)   Work study and demand forecasting   Determine Job Requirements   Training & Development Prog   Selection Procedure   Recruitment Plan

11. A brief explanation of the steps on the manpower planning process is given below :- 1. Objectives of HR Planning :

According to Sikulaq, A.F. (1978), "the ultimate purpose of HR planning is to relate future human resources future enterprise needs so as to maximise the future return on investment in human resources". HR planning is an integral part of he corporate planning.

It must be integrated with the overall organisational plans. HR planning should be more concerned with filling future vacancies with right type of people rather than with matching existing personnel with existing jobs. 2. Current HR inventory : Study of current HR supply may be undertaken by department, by function, by occupation, or by level of skill or qualifications.

Assessment of demand for the operative personnel presents less problems of uncertainty but projections of HR requirement for supervisory and managerial levels presents a complex problem because the required talents are not available at a short notice. This justifies the need to ascertain the present HR inventory in the enterprise. This will also help in drawing recruitment and development plans to meet the needs of certain skills in the future. Systematic steps must be taken in order o ensure that a resource of talent is available when vacancies occur. The search for talented employees in the organisation must be continuous. To be sure that available talent has been included, the inventory of various skills in the enterprise should be indexed. Detailed bio-data of each individual included in HR inventory must be obtained separately for the purpose of manpower planning.

Human Resource Planning

Human Resource Management is very important for the survival and prosperity of an organisation. Procurement of right kind and right number of employees is the first operative function of Human Resource Management.

Before selecting the right man for the right job, it becomes necessary to determine the quality and quantity of people required in the organisation. This is the primary function of Human Resource Planning.

Human Resource Planning is the planning of Human Resources. It is also called manpower planning/ personnel planning/ employment planning. It is only after Human Resource Planning that the Human Resource department can initiate the recruitment and selection process. Therefore Human Resource Planning is a sub-system of organisational planning.

Definition

"Human Resource Planning is a strategy for the acquisition, utilisation, improvement and preservation of an organisation's human resource" – Y.C. Moushell

"Human Resource Planning is a process of forecasting an organisation's future demand for human resource and supply of right type of people in right numbers" – J.Chennly.K

Features of Human Resource Planning

1. It is future oriented: – Human Resource Planning is forward-looking. It involves forecasting the manpower needs for a future

period so that adequate and timely provisions may be made to meet the needs.

2. It is a continuous process: – Human Resource Planning is a continuous process because the demand and supply of Human Resource keeps fluctuating throughout the year. Human Resource Planning has to be reviewed according to the needs of the organisation and changing environment.

3. Integral part of Corporate Planning: – Manpower planning is an integral part of corporate planning because without a corporate plan there can be no manpower planning.

4. Optimum utilisation of resources: – The basic purpose of Human Resource Planning is to make optimum utilisation of organisation's current and future human resources.

5. Both Qualitative and Quantitative aspect: – Human Resource Planning considers both the qualitative and quantitative aspects of Human Resource Management, 'Quantitative' meaning the right number of people and 'Qualitative' implying the right quality of manpower required in the organisation.

6. Long term and Short term: – Human Resource Planning is both Long-term and short-term in nature. Just like planning which is long-term and short-term depending on the need of the hour, Human Resource Planning keeps long-term goals and short-term goals in view while predicting and forecasting the demand and supply of Human Resource. Involves study of manpower requirement: – Human Resource Planning involves the study of

manpower availability and the manpower requirement in the organisation.

Objectives of Human Resource Planning

1. Optimum utilisation of human resources currently employed in the organisation.
2. To reduce imbalance in distribution and allocation of manpower in organisation for various activities.
3. To ensure that the organisation is well-equipped with the required Quantity and Quality of manpower on a sustained basis.
4. To anticipate the impact of technology on jobs and resources.
5. To control cost of Human Resources employed, used and maintained in the organisation.
6. To provide a basis for management development programmes.
7. To ensure optimum contribution and satisfaction of the personnel with reasonable expenditure.
8. To recruit and retain human resource of required Quantity and Quality.

Need for Human Resource Planning

1. Shortage of Skills: – These days we find shortage of skills in people. So it is necessary to plan for such skilled people much in advance than when we actually need them. Non-availability of skilled people when and where they are needed is an important factor which prompts sound Human Resource Planning.
2. Frequent Labour Turnover: – Human Resource Planning is essential because of frequent labour turnover which is unavoidable by all means. Labour turnover arises because of

discharges, marriages, promotion, transfer etc which causes a constant ebb and flow in the workforce in the organisation.

3. Changing needs of technology: – Due to changes in technology and new techniques of production, existing employees need to be trained or new blood injected into an organisation.

4. Identify areas of surplus or shortage of personnel: – Manpower planning is needed in order to identify areas with a surplus of personnel or areas in which there is a shortage of personnel. If there is a surplus, it can be re-deployed, or if there is a shortage new employees can be procured.

5. Changes in organisation design and structure: – Due to changes in organisation structure and design we need to plan the required human resources right from the beginning.

Problems with Human Resource Planning

1. Resistance by Employers: – Many employers resist Human Resource Planning as they think that it increases the cost of manpower for the management. Further, employers feel that Human Resource Planning is not necessary as candidates will be available as and when required in the country due to the growing unemployment situation.

2. Resistance by Employees: – Employees resist Human Resource Planning as it increases the workload on the employees and prepares programmes for securing human resources mostly from outside.

3. Inadequacies in quality of information: – Reliable information about the economy, other industries, labour markets, trends in

human resources etc are not easily available. This leads to problems while planning for human resources in the organisation.

4. Uncertainties: – Uncertainties are quite common in human resource practices in India due to absenteeism, seasonal unemployment, labour turnover etc. Further, the uncertainties in the industrial scenario like technological changes and marketing conditions also cause imperfection in Human Resource Planning. It is the uncertainties that make Human Resource Planning less reliable.

5. Time and expense: – Human Resource Planning is a time-consuming and expensive exercise. A good deal of time and cost are involved in data collection and forecasting.

Guidelines for making Human Resource Planning effective

1. Adequate information system: – The main problem faced in Human Resource Planning is the lack of information. So an adequate Human resource database should be maintained/developed for better coordinated and more accurate Human Resource Planning.

2. Participation: – To be successful, Human Resource Planning requires active participation and coordinated efforts on the part of operating executives. Such participation will help to improve understanding of the process and thereby, reduce resistance from the top management.

3. Adequate organisation: – Human Resource Planning should be properly organised; a separate section or committee may be

constituted within the human resource department to provide adequate focus and to coordinate the planning efforts at various levels.

4. Human Resource Planning should be balanced with corporate planning: – Human resource plans should be balanced with the corporate plans of the enterprise. The methods and techniques used should fit the objectives, strategies and environment of the particular organisation.

5. Appropriate time horizon: – The period of manpower plans should be appropriate according to the needs and circumstances of the specific enterprise. The size and structure of the enterprise as well as the changing aspirations of the people should be taken into consideration.

Factors affecting Human Resource Plans

External factor:

They are the factors which affect the Human Resource Planning externally. They include:-

1. Government policies: – Policies of the government like labour policy, industrial policy, policy towards reserving certain jobs for different communities and sons-of-the-soil etc affect Human Resource Planning.

2. Level of economic development: – Level of economic development determines the level of human resource development in the country and thereby the supply of human resources in the future in the country.

3. Information Technology: – Information technology brought amazing shifts in the way business operates. These shifts include business process reengineering, enterprise resource planning and Supply Chain Management. These changes brought unprecedented reduction in human resource and increase in software specialists. Example: – Computer-aided design (CAD) and computer-aided technology (CAT) also reduced the existing requirement of human resource.

4. Level of Technology: – Technology is the application of knowledge to practical tasks which lead to new inventions and discoveries. The invention of the latest technology determines the kind of human resources required.

5. Business Environment: – Business environment means the internal and external factors influencing the business. Business environmental factors influences the volume of mix of production and thereby the supply of human resources in the future in the country.

6. International factors: – International factors like the demand and supply of Human resources in various countries also affects Human Resource Planning .

Internal factors:

1. Company Strategies: – The organisation's policies and strategies relating to expansion, diversification etc. determines the human resource demand in terms of Quantity and Quality

2. Human Resource policies: – Human Resource policies of the company regarding quality of human resources, compensation

level, quality of working conditions etc. influence Human Resource Planning.

3. Job analysis: – Job analysis means detailed study of the job including the skills needed for a particular job. Human Resource Planning is based on job analysis which determines the kind of employees to be procured.

4. Time Horizon: – Company's planning differs according to the competitive environment i.e. companies with stable competitive environment can plan for the long run whereas firms without a stable environment can only plan for short term. Therefore, when there are many competitors entering business/ when there is rapid change in social and economic conditions of business/ if there is constant change in demand patterns/ when there exists poor management practice, then short term planning is adopted or vice-versa for long-term planning.

5. Type and Quality of Information: – Any planning process needs qualitative and accurate information about the organisational structure, capital budget, functional area objectives, level of technology being used, job analysis, recruitment sources, retirement plans, compensation levels of employees etc. Therefore Human Resource Planning is determined on the basis of the type and quality of information.

6. Company's production and operational policy: – Company's policies regarding how much to produce and how much to purchase from outside in order to manufacture the final product influences the number and kind of people required.

7. Trade Unions: – If the unions declare that they will not work for more than 8 hours a day, it affects the Human Resource Planning. Therefore influence of trade unions regarding the number of working hours per week, recruitment sources etc. Affect Human Resource Planning.

8. Organisational Growth Cycles: – At starting stage the organisation is small and the need of employees is usually smaller, but when the organisation enters the growth phase more young people need to be hired. Similarly, in the declining/recession/downturn phase Human Resource Planning is done to re-trench the employees.

Important Aspects of Human Resource Planning or SHRM

Planning an organization's human resources strategy often involves linking the practical aspects of employee management with the more lofty goals of coordinating services across the business's various functions. According to author John Bratton, "Strategic human resource management is the process of linking the human resource function with the strategic objectives of the organization in order to improve performance." Understanding the important aspects of SHRM can enable a business to tailor its employee and resource plans to meet its most pressing needs.

HR Practices and Performances

One of the foundational beliefs of strategic human resource management is that aligning HR strategy with the organization's overall business strategy helps to improve performance and leads to the business becoming more competitive in the marketplace.

Therefore, SHRM seeks to initiate organization-wide practices that lead to increased employee motivation, decreased reliance on hierarchies of management and an increased push for performance data to measure employee progress. An organization might, for instance, institute an employee compensation plan that rewards increased productivity with extended vacation time or flexible working hours.

Designing Workflow Processes

SHRM stresses the importance of organizational design and its impact on employee and resource planning. This often involves the cultivation of soft skills that encourage what Bratton calls "the vertical and horizontal compression of tasks and greater work autonomy." Developing high-performance work systems and encouraging managers to be committed to carrying out the organization's goals and objectives can go far in developing a flattened hierarchy where employees are encouraged to voice their opinions and give feedback on what is and isn't working within their daily processes.

Workplace Learning

SHRM also recognizes the value of establishing workplace learning programs to help employees and managers achieve the business's goals. Sometimes called professional development or training initiatives, workplace learning teaches employees to commit to a plan of action, to be flexible in their work approaches and to aim for high quality in their outputs.

This learning can be either formal, as in training seminars or higher education courses, or informal in which training is integrated as part of the mentoring process between employees and managers. Both types of learning can strengthen the business's core competencies, which include the skills and attitudes that set it apart from the competition.

Fostering Leadership and Teamwork

Leadership is the process of transforming employee behaviors and attitudes so that they better align with the organization's mission and with the employees' individual strengths. Unlike management, leadership is a more organic process and is not necessarily concerned with hierarchy or strict planning regimes. SHRM is specifically interested in empowering employees at all levels of the organization to exhibit respect for one another, open communication and pride in their work, and to express opinions rationally and objectively. The idea is that increased leadership leads to a higher level of teamwork, which in turns leads to increased productivity.

Human Resource Planning Process Or Steps Of HR Planning

Human resource planning is a process through which the company anticipates future business and environmental forces. Human resources planning assess the manpower requirement for future period of time. It attempts to provide sufficient manpower required to perform organizational activities. HR planning is a continuous process which starts with identification of HR objectives, move through analysis of manpower resources and ends at appraisal of HR planning. Following are the major steps involved in human resource planning:

1. Assessing Human Resources

The assessment of HR begins with environmental analysis, under which the external (PEST) and internal (objectives, resources and structure) are analyzed to assess the currently available HR inventory level. After the analysis of external and internal forces of the organization, it will be easier for HR manager to find out the internal strengths as well as weakness of the organization in one hand and opportunities and threats on the other. Moreover, it includes an inventory of the workers and skills already available within the organization and a comprehensive job analysis.

2. Demand Forecasting

HR forecasting is the process of estimating demand for and supply of HR in an organization. Demand forecasting is a process of determining future needs for HR in terms of quantity and quality. It is done to meet the future personnel requirements of the organization to achieve the desired level of output. Future human resource need can be estimated with the help of the organization's current human resource situation and analysis of organizational plans an procedures. It will be necessary to perform a year-by-year analysis for every significant level and type.

3. Supply Forecasting

Supply is another side of human resource assessment. It is concerned with the estimation of supply of manpower given the analysis of current resource and future availability of human resource in the organization. It estimates the future sources of HR that are likely to be available from within an outside the organization. Internal source includes promotion, transfer, job enlargement and enrichment, whereas external source includes recruitment of fresh candidates who are capable of performing well in the organization.

4. Matching Demand And Supply

It is another step of human resource planning. It is concerned with bringing the forecast of future demand and supply of HR. The matching process refers to bring demand and supply in an equilibrium position so that shortages and over staffing position will be solved. In case of shortages an organization has to hire more required number of employees. Conversely, in the case of over staffing it has to reduce the level of existing employment. Hence, it is concluded that this matching process gives knowledge about requirements and sources of HR.

5. Action Plan

It is the last phase of human resource planning which is concerned with surplus and shortages of human resource. Under it, the HR plan is executed through the designation of different HR activities. The major activities which are required to execute the HR plan are recruitment, selection, placement, training and development, socialization etc. Finally, this step is followed by control and evaluation of performance of HR to check whether the HR planning matches the HR objectives and policies. This action plan should be updated according to change in time ans conditions.

Steps in the Human Resource Planning Process
8 processes of human resource planning

Human resource (HR) planning or manpower planning is a continuous process. The human resource manager is required to revise the employment policies from time to time for achieving the best results. Human resource planning/ manpower planning process involve the following steps:-

1. Objectives of human resource planning: human resource planning must be matched with overall organizational plans. It should be concerned with filling future vacancies rather than matching existing personnel with existing jobs.

2. Current manpower stock: Current manpower stock must be continuously maintained by every department. Manpower inventory must have the detailed bio data of each individual . this record not only help in employee development but also in the finding out the surplus/ shortage of manpower.

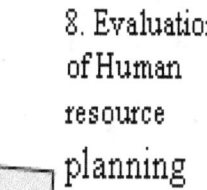
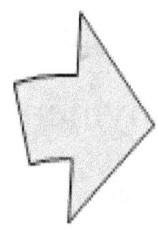

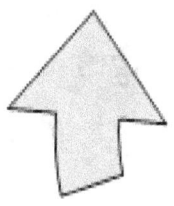

8. Evaluation of Human resource planning

1 objectives of human resource planning

2. Current manpower stock

7. Training and development

3. Demand/ supply forecasting

6. Employment programme

5. Redeployment and redundancy

4. Determining net requirement

3. Demand/ supply forecasting: firstly the organization must check the demand of manpower after every one year, two-year so on. For this purposeemployment trends to show the number of employees on payroll during last say three years to show the trend.

Replacement needs arise due to the death, retirement or termination of the employees. Growth and expansion helps in creating a number of positions at work place. After the demand forecasting it is also important to check the supply of the different type of personnel for this purpose human resource audit, replacement charts can be prepared.

4. Determining net requirement: human resource manager must check the demand and supply of the manpower before deriving at any conclusion.

5. Redeployment and redundancy: in redeployment the surplus employees in one department can be transferred to another department where deficit of employees estimated and in case of redundancy where surplus employees can not be redeployed they can be offered voluntary retirement scheme.

6. Employment programme: here it is required to prepare programmes of recruitment, selection, transfer and promotion to achieve organization goal.

7. Training and development: it is very necessary for the employees to keep them updated in the job they are doing.

8. Evaluation of Human resource planning: after doing all the above steps it is necessary to evaluate the effectiveness of human resource planning.

Thus, the above mentioned steps are important steps for the process of human resource planning.

CHAPTER – 5
INTRODUCTION TO
HUMAN RESOURCE DEVELOPMENT

The achievement of sustained and equitable development remains the greatest challenge facing the human race.Despite go od progress over the past generation, more than 1 billion people still live in acute poverty and suffer grossly inadequate access to the resources-education, health services, infrastructure, and credit-required to give them a chance of a better life. The essential task of development is to provide opportunities so that these people and hundreds of millions not much better off, can reach their potential. World Bank, 1992 . The world has progressed in many unique ways and directions in the last three decades. It has developed technologically, economically and industrially. It also richerin terms of human capabilities, facilities and quality of living. Improvements in education, communication, technology and markets have made the world a global village.

People live longer today, are better informed, can communi cate with one another across theworld and therefore carry on eco nomic, professional, educational, social and other activities with ease. These decades of development indicate the vast potential for creating a world of order, security and well -being.

The developments ofthe last three decades also indicate that while remarkable progress has been made in a number of directions, the fruits of development have not benefited the world's growing number of poor people. And where some people. And where some benefits have reached the poor, new pr oblems are appearing in the form of deteriorating social fabric and environmental degradation.

The world faces two major development challenges. The first is to ensure that the fruits of development reach the neediest through equitable distribution of resources, opportunities and be nefits. The second is to develop human capabilities and address the challenges of development political, economic and social. The few countries that have been able to meet both these Challenges have demonstrated the importance of investing in developing people and improving the quality of their life through the adoption of human resource development strategies.

THE CONTEXT AND THE NEED FOR HUMAN RESOURCE DEVELOPMENT

Today, there is practically no government or international agency that does not see theimportance of humanresource deve lopment. The World Bank;the United Nations and its constituent bodies include UNDP,UNIDO, WHO, ILO, UNICEF, UNESC, UNFPA, UNESCAP; regional bodies like ASEAN and SAARC; TheSouth Commission; theCommonwealth Secretariat; internati onal non-government organizations(NGO's);

and bilateral aid agencies, all recognize the need for , and the importance of, human resource development. Thecomponents and dimensions of human resource development which they perc eive as being of strategic importance at a given point of time, for a given country or group of countries, may vary, but the focus is uniform.

The context for the renewed emphasis on human resource d evelopment is significant. The structural adjustments program mers adopted in a number of countries have brought home the vulnerability of human development variables. The link ages between investments in human development programmes a nd economic development have become sharper.

There have been major international developments-such as the opening ofglobal markets, the increased market orientation o f economies and the restructuring in socialist countries-which have given rise toan increased competition, forcing developing c ountries to produce and market quality products at competitive prices. At the same time a range of concerns, including envir onmental issues, the changing role of women, the new inform ation culture and demands for liberalization and democracy, are influencing policy and practice.

Human Resource Development

Human Resource Development is the part of human resource management that specifically deals with training and development of the employees in the organization. Human resource development includes training a person after he or she is first hired, providing opportunities to learn new skills, distributing resources that are beneficial for the employee's tasks, and any other developmental activities.

Introduction to HRM

- Human Resource Management
- Scope of Human Resource Management
- Significance of Human Resource Management
- Human Resource Management functions
- Human Resource Management Model
- HRM Vs Personnel Management
- Human Resource Development
- Human Capital Management
- Talent Management
- Knowledge Management
- About Human Resource Manager
- HRM environment in India
- Changing role of HRM
- e-HRM

INTRODUCTION

Development of human resources is essential for any organisation that would like to be dynamic and growth-oriented. Unlike other resources, human resources have rather unlimited potential capabilities. The potential can be used only by creating a climate that can continuously identify, bring to surface, nurture and use the capabilities of people. Human Resrouce Development (HRD) system aims at creating such a climate. A number of HRD techniques have been developed in recent years to perform the above task based on certain principles. This unit provides an understanding of the concept of HRD system, related mechanisms and the changing boundaries of HRD.

HRD concept was first introduced by Leonard Nadler in 1969 in a conference in US. "He defined HRD as those learning experience which are organized, for a specific time, and designed to bring about the possibility of behavioral change".

Human Resource Development (HRD) is the framework for helping employees develop their personal and organizational skills, knowledge, and abilities. Human Resource Development includes such opportunities as employee training, employee career development, performance management and development, coaching, mentoring, succession planning, key employee identification, tuition assistance, and organization development.

The focus of all aspects of Human Resource Development is on developing the most superior workforce so that the organization and individual employees can accomplish their work goals in service to customers.

Human Resource Development can be formal such as in classroom training, a college course, or an organizational planned change effort. Or, Human Resource Development can be informal as in employee coaching by a manager. Healthy organizations believe in Human Resource Development and cover all of these bases.

Definitions of HRD

HRD (Human Resources Development) has been defined by various scholars in various ways. Some of the important definitions of HRD (Human Resources Development) are as follows:

- According to Leonard Nadler, "Human resource development is a series of organised activities, conducted within a specialised time and designed to produce behavioural changes."

- In the words of Prof. T.V. Rao, "HRD is a process by which the employees of an organisation are helped in a continuous and planned way to (i) acquire or sharpen capabilities required to perform various functions associated with their present or expected future roles; (ii) develop their journal capabilities as individual and discover and exploit their own inner potential for their own and /or organisational development purposes; (iii) develop an organisational culture in which superior-subordinate relationship, team work and collaboration among sub-units are strong and contribute to the professional well being, motivation and pride of employees." .

- According to M.M. Khan, "Human resource development is the across of increasing knowledge, capabilities and positive work attitudes of all people working at all levels in a business undertaking."

THE CONCEPT OF HUMAN RESOURCE DEVELOPMENT

Human resource development in the organisation context is a process by which the employees of an organisation are helped, in a continuous and planned way to:

1. Acquire or sharpen capabilities required to perform various functions associated with their present or expected future roles;

2. Develop their general capabilities as individuals and discover and exploit their own inner potentials for their own and/or organisational development purposes; and

3. Develop an organisational culture in which supervisor-subordinate relationships, teamwork and collaboration among sub-units are strong and contribute to the professional well being, motivation and pride of employees.

This definition of HRD is limited to the organisational context. In the context of a state or nation it would differ.

HRD is a process, not merely a set of mechanisms and techniques. The mechanisms and techniques such as performance appraisal, counselling, training, and organization development interventions are used to initiate, facilitate, and promote this process in a continuous way. Because the process has no limit, the mechanisms may need to be examined periodically to see whether they are promoting or hindering the process.

Organisations can facilitate this process of development by planning for it, by allocating organisational resources for the purpose, and by exemplifying an HRD philosophy that values human beings and promotes their development.

Difference between HRD and HRM

Both are very important concepts of management specifically related with human resources of organisation. Human resource management and human resource development can be differentiated on the following grounds:

- The human resource management is mainly maintenance oriented whereas human resource development is development oriented.

- Organisation structure in case of human resources management is independent whereas human resource development creates a structure, which is inter-dependent and inter-related.

- Human resource management mainly aims to improve the efficiency of the employees whereas aims at the development of the employees as well as organisation as a whole.

- Responsibility of human resource development is given to the personnel/human resource management department and specifically to personnel manager whereas responsibility of HRD is given to all managers at various levels of the organisation.

• HRM motivates the employees by giving them monetary incentives or rewards whereas human resource development stresses on motivating people by satisfying higher-order needs.

THE NEED FOR HRD

HRD is needed by any organisation that wants to be dynamic and growth-oriented or to succeed in a fast-changing environment. Organisations can become dynamic and grow only through the efforts and competencies of their human resources. Personnel policies can keep the morale and motivation of employees high, but these efforts are not enough to make the organisation dynamic and take it in new directions. Employee capabilities must continuously be acquired, sharpened, and used. For this purpose, an "enabling" organisational culture is essential. When employees use their initiative, take risks, experiment, innovate, and make things happen, the organisation may be said to have an "enabling" culture. Even an organisation that has reached its limit of growth, needs to adapt to the changing environment. No organisation is immune to the need for processes that help to acquire and increase its capabilities for stability and renewal.

HRD FUNCTIONS

The core of the concept of HRS is that of development of human beings, or HRD. The concept of development should cover not only the individual but also other units in the organisation. In addition to developing the individual, attention needs to be given to the development of stronger dyads, i.e., two-person groups of the employee and his boss. Such dyads are the basic units of working in the organisation. Besides several groups like committees, task groups, etc. also require attention. Development of such groups should be from the point of view of increasing collaboration amongst people working in the organisation, thus making for an effective decision-making. Finally, the entire department and the entire organisation also should be covered by development.

Their development would involve developing a climate conducive for their effectiveness, developing self-renewing mechanisms in the organisations so that they are able to adjust and pro-act, and developing relevant processes which contribute to their effectiveness.

Hence, the goals of the HRD systems are to develop:

1. The capabilities of each employee as an individual.

2. The capabilities of each individual in relation to his or her present role.

3. The capabilities of each employee in relation to his or her expected future role(s).

4. The dyadic relationship between each employee and his or her supervisor.

5. The team spirit and functioning in every organisational unit (department, group, etc.).

6. Collaboration among different units of the organisation.

7. The organisation's overall health and self-renewing capabilities which, in turn, increase the enabling capabilities of individuals, dyads, teams, and the entire organisation.

Features of Human Resource development

The essential features of human resource development can be listed as follows:

• Human resource development is a process in which employees of the organisations are recognized as its human resource. It believes that human resource is most valuable asset of the organisation.

• It stresses on development of human resources of the organisation. It helps the employees of the organisation to develop their general capabilities in relation to their present jobs and expected future role.

• It emphasise on the development and best utilization of the capabilities of individuals in the interest of the employees and organisation.

• It helps is establishing/developing better inter-personal relations. It stresses on developing relationship based on help, trust and confidence.

• It promotes team spirit among employees.

• It tries to develop competencies at the organisation level. It stresses on providing healthy climate for development in the organisation.

- HRD is a system. It has several sub-systems. All these sub-systems are inter-related and interwoven. It stresses on collaboration among all the sub-systems.

- It aims to develop an organisational culture in which there is good senior-subordinate relations, motivation, quality and sense of belonging.

- It tries to develop competence at individual, inter-personal, group and organisational level to meet organisational goal.

- It is an inter-disciplinary concept. It is based on the concepts, ideas and principles of sociology, psychology, economics etc.

- It form on employee welfare and quality of work life. It tries to examine/identify employee needs and meeting them to the best possible extent.

- It is a continuous and systematic learning process. Development is a life long process, which never ends.

Benefits of Human Resource Development

Human resource development now a days is considered as the key to higher productivity, better relations and greater profitability for any organisation. Appropriate HRD provides unlimited benefits to the concerned organisation. Some of the important benefits are being given here:

- HRD (Human Resource Development) makes people more competent. HRD develops new skill, knowledge and attitude of the people in the concern organisations.

- With appropriate HRD programme, people become more committed to their jobs. People are assessed on the basis of their performance by having a acceptable performance appraisal system.

- An environment of trust and respect can be created with the help of human resource development.

- Acceptability toward change can be created with the help of HRD. Employees found themselves better equipped with problem-solving capabilities.

- It improves the all round growth of the employees. HRD also improves team spirit in the organisation. They become more open in their behaviour. Thus, new values can be generated.

- It also helps to create the efficiency culture In the organisation. It leads to greater organisational effectiveness. Resources are properly utilised and goals are achieved in a better way.

- It improves the participation of worker in the organisation. This improve the role of worker and workers feel a sense of pride and achievement while performing their jobs.

- It also helps to collect useful and objective data on employees programmes and policies which further facilitate better human resource planning.

• Hence, it can be concluded that HRD provides a lot of benefits in every organisation. So, the importance of concept of HRD should be recognised and given a place of eminence, to face the present and future challenges in the organisation.

What is International Human Resource Management?

Human Resource Management (HRM) is set of organizational activities aimed at effectively managing and directing human resources/labour towards achieving organizational goals. Typical functions performed by HRM staff would be recruitment, selection, training and development, performance appraisal, dismissal, managing promotions and so on. Then what is International Human Resource Management (IHRM)?

IHRM can be defined as set of activities aimed managing organizational human resources at international level to achieve organizational objectives and achieve competitive advantage over competitors at national and international level.

IHRM includes typical HRM functions such as recruitment, selection, training and development, performance appraisal and dismissal done at international level and additional activities such as global skills management, expatriate management and so on.

In simple terms, IHRM is concerned about managing human resources at Multinational Companies (MNC) and it involves managing types of employees namely.

1. Home country employees- Employees belonging to home country of the firm where the corporate head quarter is situated.

2. Host country employees- Employees belonging to the nation in which the subsidiary is situated.

3. Third country employees- These are the employees who are not from home country/host country but are employed at subsidiary or corporate head quarters. As an example a American MNC which has a subsidiary at India may employ a French person as the CEO to the subsidiary. The Frenchman employed is a third country employee.

Differences between domestic HRM and International HRM (IHRM) are summarized below:

- Domestic HRM is done at national level and IHRM is done at international level.

- Domestic HRM is concerned with managing employees belonging to one nation and IHRM is concerned with managing employees belonging to many nations (Home country, host country and third country employees)

- Domestic HRM is concerned with managing limited number of HRM activities at national level and IHRM has concerned with managing additional activities such as expatriate management.

- Domestic HRM is less complicated due to less influence from the external environment. IHRM is very complicated as it is affected heavily by external factors such as cultural distance and institutional factors.

What is International Human Resource Management?

In all these MNCs or MNEs, HRM is a key to success. For the vast majority of organisations, the cost of the people who do the work is the largestsingle item of operating costs. Increasingly, in the modern world, the capabilities and the knowledge incorporated in an organisation's human resources are the key to performance. So on both the cost and benefit sides of the equation, HRM is crucial to the survival, performance and success of the enterprise.

For international organisations, the additional complications of dealing with multicultural assumptions about the way people should be managed and differing institutional constraints become important contributors to the chances of that success

CONCLUSION :

The need for human resource specialists to adopt an increasingly international orientation in the functional activities is widely acknowledged and becoming ever clearer. It is important not just to people working in the giant MNEs, but also to many in small to medium-size enterprises(SMEs).The freer economic environment of the twenty-first century,the reduction of restrictions on labour movement in are as Such as the European Union, and the advent of new technology have combined to mean that many fledgling enterprises operate internationally almost as soon as they are established. It is also worth reminding ourselves that international organizations Do not have to be in the private sector.

Governments have staff working around the world. Many international organizations such as those in the UN family, the OECD, the regional trade bodies, etc have employees working across national borders. So do many charities and religious groups.

Any review of world events over the last few years will emphasis the essentially unpredictable and rapidly changing nature of political, economic and social upheavals used the metaphor of 'permanent white water' to describe the nature of doing business in the latter part of the twentieth century:

REFERENCES
1. http//:www.google.co.in
2. http//:www.wikipedia.com